NATURE
Activity Book

ALAIN GRÉE

Button
BOOKS

The seasons

Add some stickers to these pictures of the seasons. Write the name of each season in the boxes. What is your favorite time of year?

The caterpillar's lunch

Help the caterpillar find its way through the maze to reach the tasty leaf.
Keep away from the hungry birds!

A traditional tale

Choose words from the sticker pages to finish this story.

One day a beautiful but vain peacock met a sparrow on a dusty road. To show off

to the sparrow, the peacock spread his lovely [ ], which shone like the

sun. The peacock said, "Look at me. I am dressed like a king. I am wearing all the colors

of the [ ] while your feathers are as brown as dirt! What can you do?"

The [ ] then spread his strong [ ] and flew up to the sun.

"Follow me if you can," he said. But the peacock stood where he was in the dust, while the

sparrow escaped into the [ ] sky.

Tall trees

Do the math to find out which of these trees will grow the tallest. Can you match the nuts and leaves to the trees? Draw lines to link them.

horse chestnut

$15 + 4 + 8$

$= \bigcirc$

pine

$13 - 2 + 9$

$= \bigcirc$

oak

$8 + 7 + 10$

$= \bigcirc$

The story of an apple

Number the pictures and captions to show how the seeds of an apple can grow into a new tree. Some have been done for you. How many apples are in the big basket on the opposite page? Write your answer in the circle, then draw some more trees if you like.

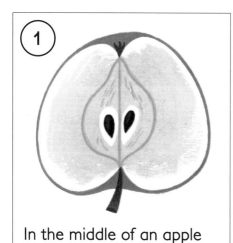

(1) In the middle of an apple are the core and pips.

( ) In spring, pink and white flowers come out.

( ) In late summer, they ripen into lovely fruit.

( ) Plant an apple seed in the ground and water it.

( ) In fall, the apples are ready for picking.

( ) The shoot grows. It forms the stem and leaves.

(7) During summer, the fruits grow.

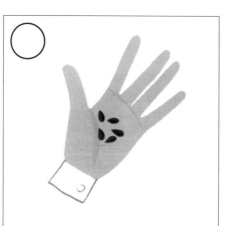

( ) The pips in the apple are apple seeds.

( ) The plant grows into a tree.

There are apples in this basket. ◯

Animal footprints

Each footprint belongs to a different animal. From the tracks, can you tell which one reaches the cozy cabin, the woodpile, and the sled? Write the names in the boxes.

rabbit

bird

dog

Looking in a rock pool

This girl is looking in a rock pool to find some small sea creatures.
Put a check in the circle by the ones she is most likely to find.

Nature counting

How many of the following can you see in the picture? Add some stickers of more bluebirds and ladybugs if you like.

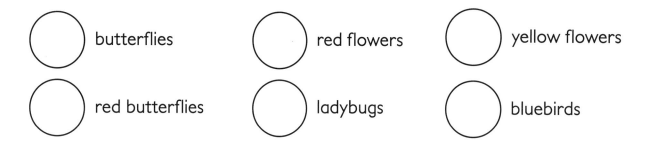

( ) butterflies   ( ) red flowers   ( ) yellow flowers

( ) red butterflies   ( ) ladybugs   ( ) bluebirds

Matching snails

Link the snails to each other to make matching pairs. How many pairs of snails are there?

◯ pairs of snails

Hungry birds

Which bird ate the most seeds? Do the math to find out. Write the numbers in the circles, then color in the birds.

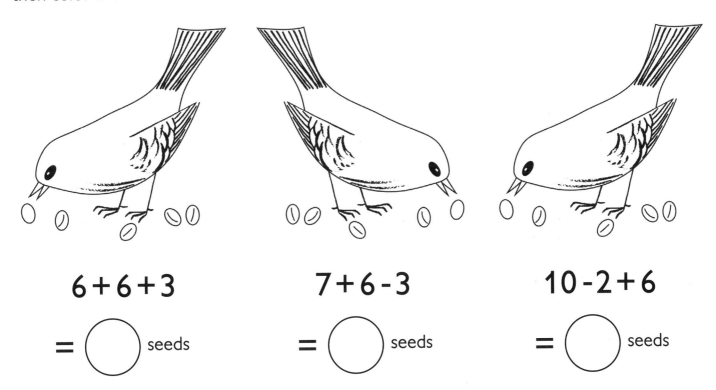

6 + 6 + 3

= ◯ seeds

7 + 6 - 3

= ◯ seeds

10 - 2 + 6

= ◯ seeds

Butterfly shadows

Match each butterfly to its shadow by drawing lines between them.

Springtime scene

Can you spot five differences between these two pictures?

Egg heads

Next time you have a boiled egg, keep the shell and use it to make
a character with hair that grows.

1. Carefully wash the empty eggshell – don't break it! Draw a little face on your shell as shown using felt-tip pens.

2. Place a damp cotton ball inside the shell.

3. Gently add some alfalfa or wheatgrass seeds.

4. Photocopy the pieces opposite and color them in, or you can design and decorate your own using the shapes as a guide.

5. Roll the body piece around and glue it in place to form an open-topped cone. Use paper clips to hold it in place while the glue dries.

6. Place your eggshell on top of the cone body as shown below, then place it in a sunny spot, such as on a windowsill. Check every evening that the cotton ball is still damp and add water if it needs it. In a few days, your little egg head will have sprouted some funny green hair!

Alfalfa will grow into curly hair, wheatgrass into straighter hair.

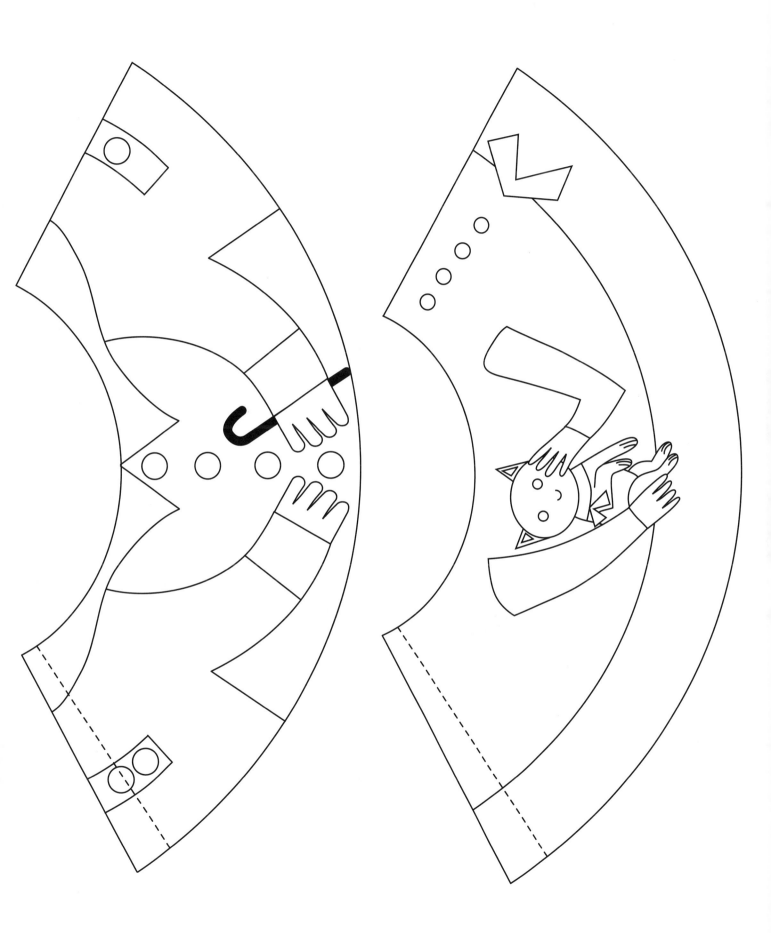

The weather

Choose a word from the list that describes the weather in each picture and write it in the boxes. Color in the final picture and add some more weather features if you like.

snow

fog

rain

lightning

sunshine

wind

Animal mix-up

These animals have gotten their names in a muddle. Write their names in the boxes.

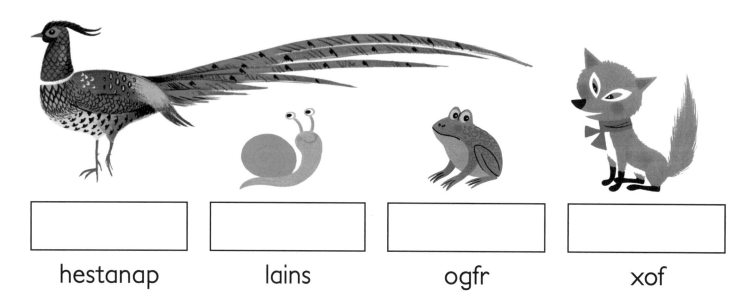

hestanap	lains	ogfr	xof

Find the feeder

Fill in the missing letters to find out the names of these birds. Then follow the tangled lines to find out which one will find its way to the garden feeder.

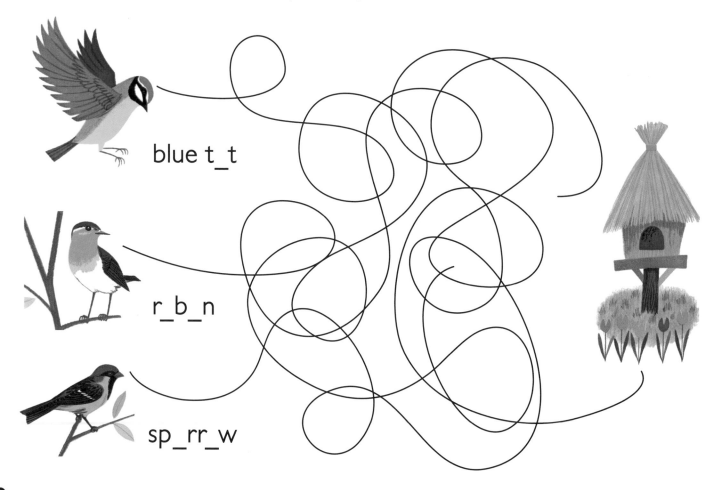

blue t_t

r_b_n

sp_rr_w

Dotty girl

Join the dots to show this girl collecting flowers, then color in the picture.
Add some stickers of flowers and butterflies if you like.

Sounds of nature

How many sounds can you hear in the countryside? Match the sounds with the pictures by drawing a line between them.

What other animal sounds can you think of? Write them here.

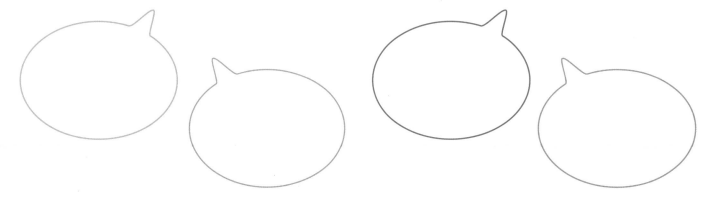

Animals with stripes

These animals are losing their stripes! Can you help by coloring them back in?

Bird sticker fun

Can you use the stickers to put these birds back together
again? Some are missing their heads, some their tails.
Then use more stickers to add extra birds to the tree.

Busy bees

Join the dots to complete this picture of a bee collecting pollen. Then do the math to find out which bee will collect the most pollen and write your answers in the circles below. When you've done that, color everything in.

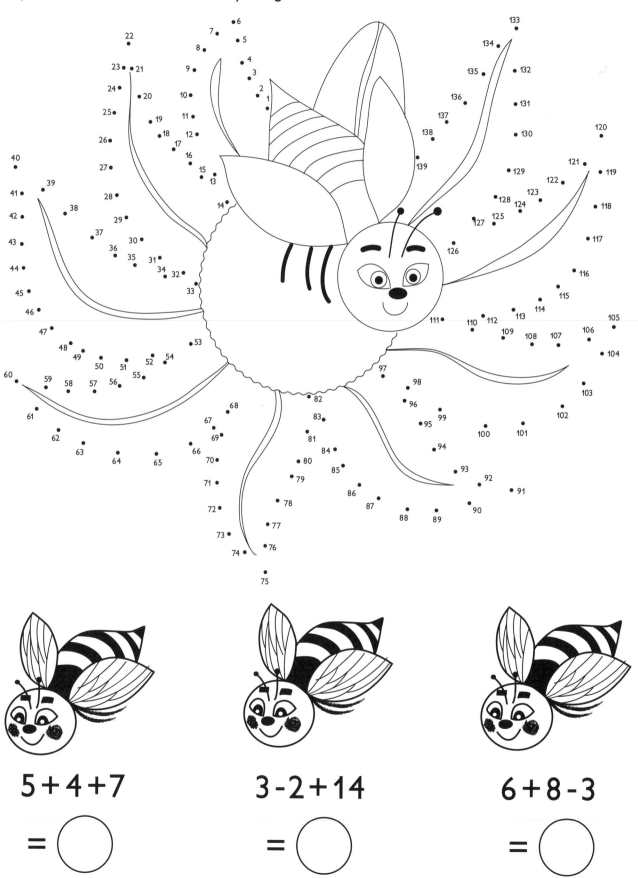

$5 + 4 + 7$

$= \bigcirc$

$3 - 2 + 14$

$= \bigcirc$

$6 + 8 - 3$

$= \bigcirc$

Garden birds

Can you find all the words in the puzzle?

sparrow   crow
thrush   finch
warbler   starling
blackbird   dove
woodpecker robin

```
s b l a c k b i r d s w
s t v n l f w c e z p o
t h r u s h i a s w a o
a t e r r b w h c h r d
r l f b l q a x e c r p
l x i d r c r o w n o e
i e n c o b b k e i w c
n h c u b h l g i f y k
g r h x i y e d o v e e
k o c j n b r f w c f r
```

Watering the plants

This boy is watering the plants, but only one is getting enough water. Which one is it? Follow the tangled lines to find out.

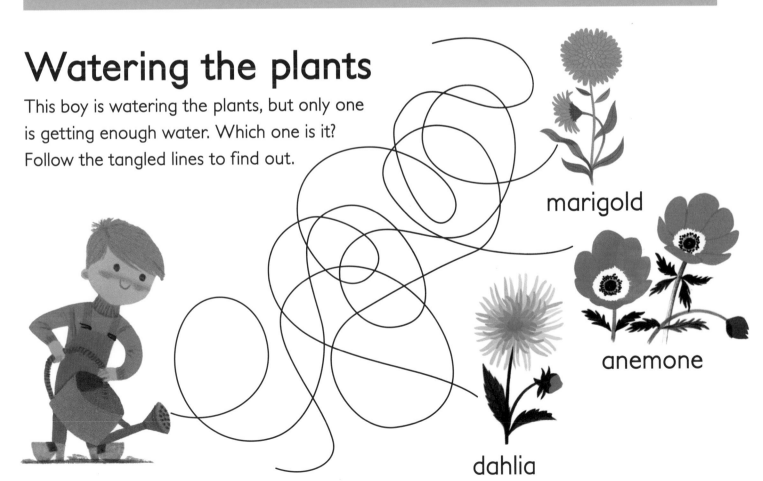

marigold

anemone

dahlia

Butterfly life cycle

Use the circle below to show the life cycle of a butterfly in the right order. Write the words in the boxes and add the correct stickers from the center of the book.

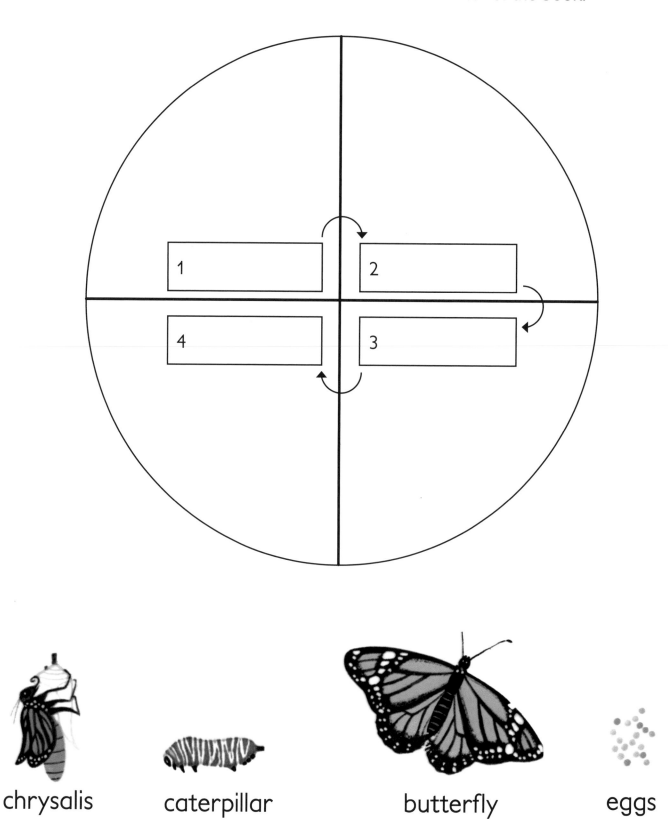

chrysalis   caterpillar   butterfly   eggs

Growing plants

What do plants need to make them grow? Put a check in the circle by all the things that you think will help them grow. Then draw some plants in the greenhouse.

Ladybug maze

Can you help this ladybug find her way to the sunflower? Avoid the spider and the toad!

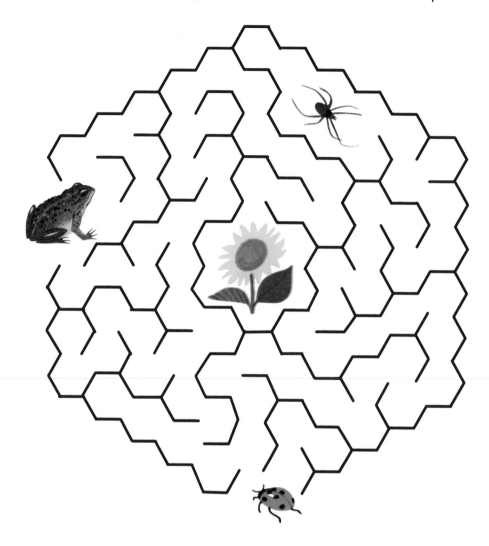

Nature jokes

Q: What do you call a cow that eats your grass?
A: A lawn moo-er.

Q: Why did the leaf go to the doctor?
A: It was feeling green.

Q: What's the biggest moth in the world?
A: A mammoth.

Q: What kind of tree can you grow in your hand?
A: A palm tree.

Dotty lion

Join the dots to find this king of the jungle then color him in.

Odd one out

Which of these birds is the odd one out?

Woodland friends

Count the animals in the picture. Then add some more creatures using the stickers.

( ) frogs ( ) rabbits ( ) mice

( ) squirrels ( ) snails ( ) bears

Which of these animals...

...hibernate for winter?

...are good jumpers?

...have antennae?

Word games

Complete these words using the letters from the word winter.

sno _

m _ ttens

sca _ f

ha _

tr _ e

carrot _ ose

Crab matching

Which one of these crabs matches the silhouette?

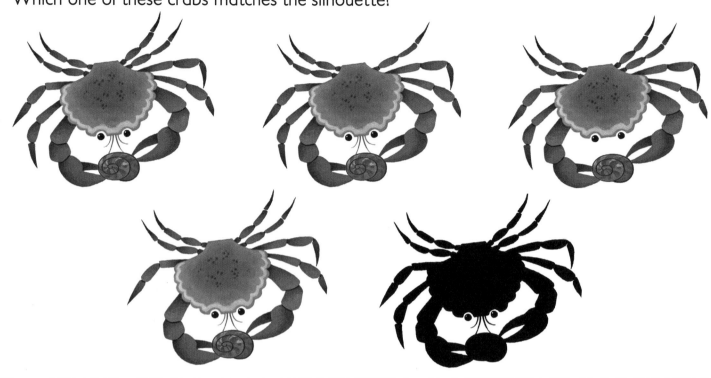

Forest friends

Can you find all the forest animals hidden in the puzzle?

squirrel	owl
bear	fox
rabbit	snail
mouse	deer
wolf	bird

```
y u s b d f o x u p y l
h g n i e e d r b q w s
s o r r t a e s e s c q
b c n d e f e r a n t u
e s e r b u r b r a p i
a s a r a b b i t i r r
r e u r w o l f e l h r
b c r o u w o u r l i e
q e s n m o u s e u f l
l e c c l j q o w l y p
```

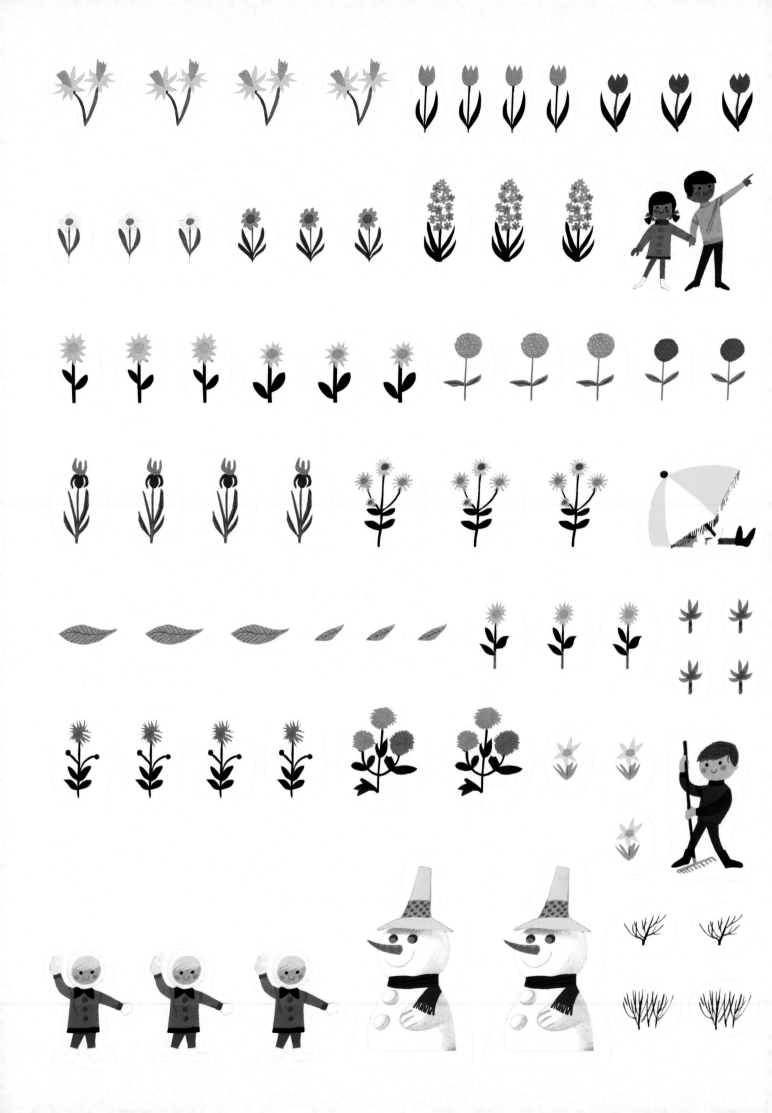

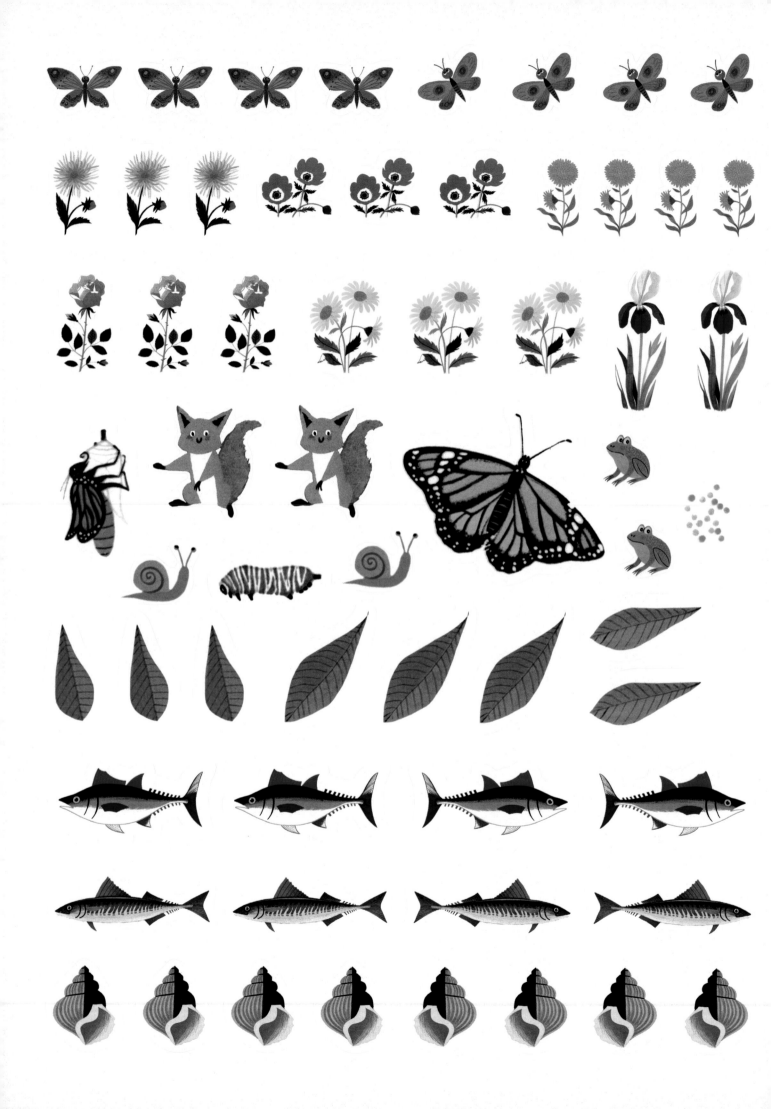

A traditional tale

| blue | wings | tail | sparrow | rainbow |

The old oak tree

robin	happy	eggs	branches	tree
friends	hole	night	birds	winter
squirrel				

Animal riddles

| snail | spider | giraffe | monkey | bee |
| snake | | | | |

Hidden acorns

These squirrels have buried their acorns under different trees. Follow the tangled line from each squirrel to help them find their store.

pine

oak

birch

On which tree do acorns grow? Write your answer below.

Raking up leaves

Can you spot five differences between these two scenes?

Where do they live?

Which of these creatures live on the ground and which in trees? Write the names underneath each list heading at the bottom of the page.

wild boar

gibbon

woodpecker

fox

robin

squirrel

tortoise

elephant

On the ground

_____

_____

_____

_____

In trees

_____

_____

_____

_____

Back to the hive

Can you help this bee get back to the honeycomb through the maze?

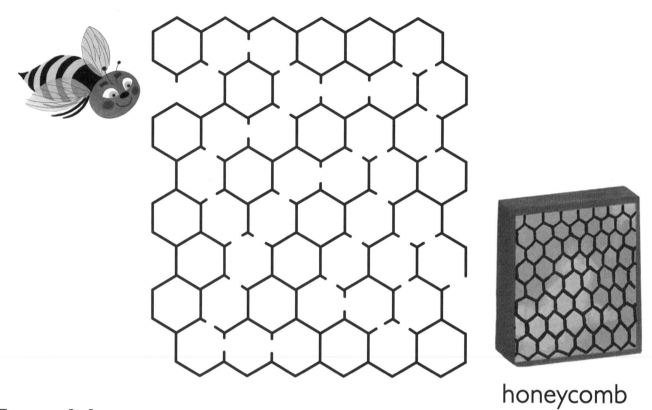

honeycomb

Food in nature

Can you name the natural food sources on the top row and the foods on the bottom row? Then draw a line to show which are connected. One has been done for you.

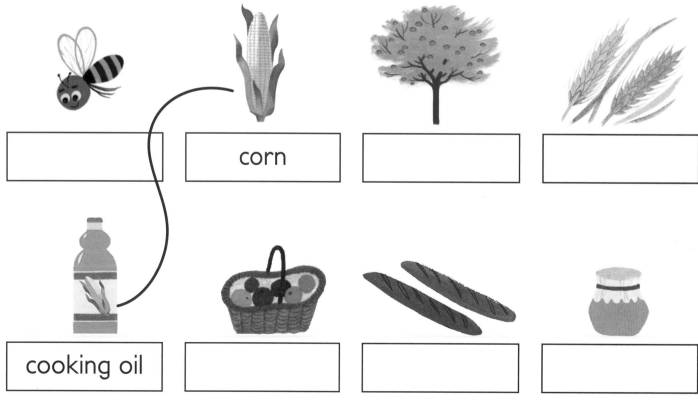

corn

cooking oil

Spotting sea birds

Can you work out which of these sea birds is being described below?

1. Which bird has a brightly colored beak, pink legs, and lives in a burrow?

2. Which bird lives near the South Pole and can be over 1m tall?

3. Which black and white bird lives most of its life at sea?

4. Which long-necked bird holds its wings out to dry?

5. Which noisy bird has an orange beak and legs and lives in seaside towns?

puffin

seagull

guillemot

emperor penguin

cormorant

Summer view

How many flowers can you see in this picture? How many apples are there in the tree? Write your answers in the circles below.

flowers

apples

Fruit jumble

Unscramble the names of the fruits and write them in the boxes below. Draw a circle around the fruits you think grow on trees.

serap

brasseprier

nasgore

spepla

rebrisawters

echirrse

molens

Fish and shellfish

If you look at creatures in a rock pool or the sea, you will notice that some have shells and others don't. Which creatures below are fish and which are shellfish? Circle the ones that you think are shellfish, then color them all in.

shrimp

sole

crab

lobster

tuna

cod

The old oak tree

Choose words from the sticker pages to finish this story.

An old oak [_____] sat in the forest feeling very sorry for

himself. "I'm no use to anyone," he sighed. "I've got knots in my trunk,

my [_____] are all twisted, and there's a pain in my fork where

the water's coming in. I'm so sad and lonely. Boo hoo!"

One dark and stormy [_____] , a branch blew off and left a big [_____]

in the oak tree's trunk. Soon, a little [_____] spotted it. "Hallo, Mr. Oak! I've been

looking for somewhere to spend the [_____] . That hole looks perfect for me and

my family," she said. May we stay with you?"

"Of course," said the oak tree. "It would be a pleasure." So the squirrel built her nest.

In the spring, a chirpy [_____] perched on a high branch. "Hallo, Mr. Oak! Look

at all your lovely branches! There's room for me and all my [_____] to build our

nests. Please can we come and stay with you?"

"Of course," replied the old oak. Soon there were lots of [_____] in the tree,

building nests and laying their [_____] .

The old oak tree was very [_____] .

"I guess I'm not so useless after all," he said.

"And I'll never be lonely again!"

Underwater life

Join the dots to find the starfish, then color it in. Then add some stickers to this underwater scene.

Sink or swim?

Put a check in the circles by the animals that you think are good swimmers. Can you think of any others? Write their names in the space below.

penguin

zebra

goldfish

sheep

parrot

frog

duck

sea lion

cow

Other swimmers

_____   _____

_____   _____

Fading flowers

Color in the other halves of these flower pictures. Which one has the most petals?

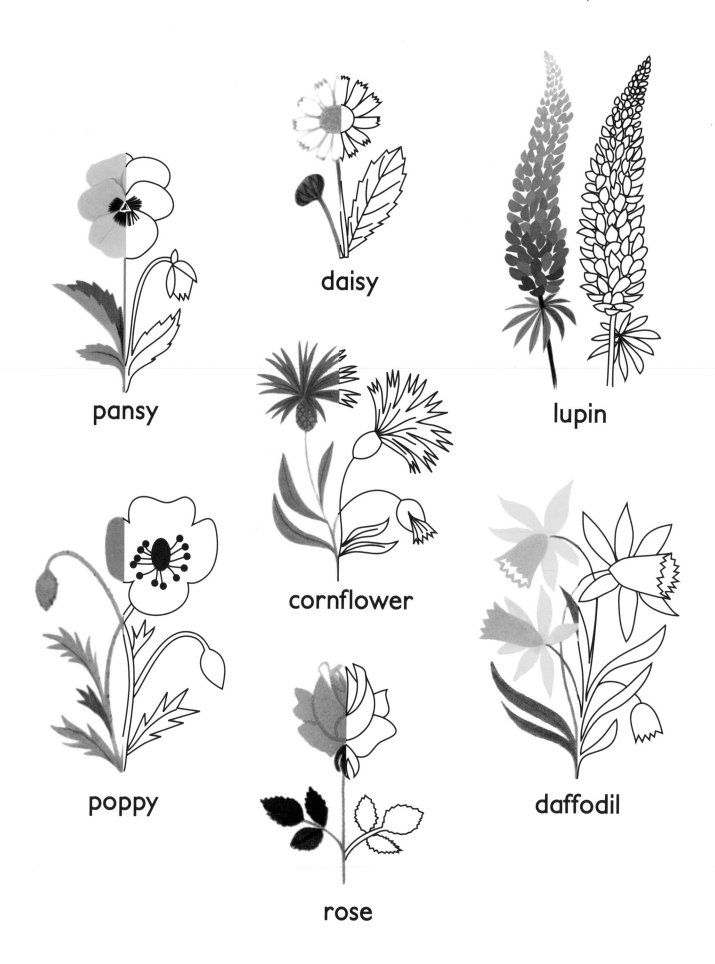

pansy

daisy

lupin

cornflower

poppy

daffodil

rose

Animal riddles

Solve these riddles to identify each animal. Choose words from the sticker pages to finish each riddle, or write them in.

1. I'm tall, I have a long neck, I eat leaves. Who am I?

2. I slither, I hiss, I have a scaly coat. Who am I?

3. I'm small, I'm striped, I have wings. Who am I?

4. I spin a web, I'm small, I'm hairy. Who am I?

5. I can climb, I have hands, I live in trees. Who am I?

6. I'm small, I'm slow, I leave a slimy trail. Who am I?

On the seashore

What can you find on the seashore in this puzzle?

crab
gull
pebble
lobster
octopus

rocks
seaweed
shells
shrimp
starfish

```
e s d s c g z o s i t s
p t u e u u c q h e w g
e a i a e l n s r m o b
b r l w o l l h i c c p
b f r e f b a l m r t o
l i u e e l u e p a o g
e s h d a l s y s b p x
f h s r j g a b h c u w
d i v l o b s t e r s i
h s h e l l s n n g h h
g d g h w m s t l h y k
r o c k s c g p k j o t
```

Fall coloring

Color in this scene and add stickers. How many leaves are on the ground?

Ocean safety

The ocean is a fun place to be, but you need to take care. Circle the answers you think will keep you and the wildlife safe. Then color in the picture to go with the last question.

1. What do you do with a bottle on the beach?

a. I throw it into the sea.

b. I take it home with me, in case it breaks and hurts people or wildlife.

2. What do you do when you see a starfish?

a. I look at it and leave it alone.

b. I put it in my bucket and take it home.

3. What do you do with trash?

a. I bury it in the sand.

b. I put it in a trash can or I take it home.

4. Can you pour chemicals into the sea?

a. Yes, the water will wash them away.

b. No. Chemicals can poison birds and animals.

5. What should you do with sea creatures?

a. Watch them, but don't touch them.

b. I take them home with me to show to my friends.

6. What would you do with a large stone?

a. I would take it home if I liked it.

b. I would leave it where it is. Lots of tiny creatures live under large stones.

7. How do you enjoy yourself near the water?

a. I stay near an adult when paddling and swimming.

b. I go off on my own to explore.

8. How do you protect yourself when it's hot?

a. I eat ice cream.

b. I wear sunblock and a hat.

In which season?

In which season do the following things happen? Write the name of the season (spring, summer, fall or winter) in the boxes below.

...the swallow
migrates

...we build a
snowman

...the leaves
turn brown

...the bear
hibernates

...there are flowers
on an apple tree

...the days are long
and warm

Date: 09/01/20

Please find enclosed the following complimentary review copies:

Title	Author	ISBN	Price	Publisher	Pub date
Alain Grée Nature Activity Book	Alain Grée	9781787080478	$12.99	**Button Books** (an imprint of GMC Publications	April 2020
Roman Adventure Activity Book	Jen Alliston	9781787080430	$9.99	**Button Books** (an imprint of GMC Publications	April 2020
The Magical Underwater Activity Book	Mia Underwood	9781787080454	$14.99	**Button Books** (an imprint of GMC Publications	April 2020

Available from: www.thegmcgroup.com or by calling 011 44 1273 488005

If featuring a book for review/giveaway please include a high res image of the cover, title, ISBN, price, publication date, publisher info and buying link, where possible.

Please send a finished copy of any printed reviews, offers, giveaways or features to the address below. Alternatively, you can send a pdf to paul.eckersley@thegmcgroup.com

If posting on social media please tag us on 🐦**Twitter with our handle @GMCbooks OR on** 📷**Instagram under @gmcpublications**

ALSO if any reviews or exposure for these three could be planned/ scheduled until MARCH 2019 or after we would be most grateful as this will be close to when the books are available in the USA.

Paul Eckersley
Publicity Officer
GMC Distribution
The Guild of Master Craftsman
168 High Street
Lewes
BN7 1XU
United Kingdom

For further information, or to set up a feature, interview, extract, review or reader offer, please contact:

Paul Eckersley, Publicity Officer
E: paul.eckersley@thegmcgroup.com
T: 011 44 1273 402836

GMC Publications is distributed in North America by Publishers Group West.
E: info@pgw.com
T: 212-614-7888

PRESS RELEASE
Nature Activity Book

By Alain Grée

April 2020 • RRP $12.99 • For kids aged +4
Button Books

Over 100 different nature-themed activities

This delightful nature-themed activity book will entertain children who are crazy about all things to do with the great outdoors. The pages are crammed with over 100 great activities, including dot to dot, spot the difference, coloring in, simple makes and other engaging puzzles, as well as 4 pages of stickers to be used in the book.

Fun and educational, the **Nature Activity Book** features beautiful, bright illustrations that will draw children in and keep them busy. All of the pages are incredibly absorbing with Alain's unmistakably rich and appealing style of illustration. And while they are enjoying the mazes, matching and counting, the games are helping them to develop a wide range of skills, including observational, conversational and motor.

About the creator:

Alain Grée is a French author and illustrator of children's books. He has had over 300 books published, which have been translated into 20 different languages. He has also worked as a children's broadcaster on French national television, produced three detective novels, ten ship navigation books and been a journalist for 20 years for *Voiles et Voiliers* (sailing ships) magazine. He is currently a graphic designer and editor for various advertising publications. Alain's main hobby is sailing. He's owned several boats since the 1970s and has crossed the Atlantic Ocean twice. He finds his sailing trips provide the perfect time out to work on new children's stories and illustrations.

For press enquiries, review copies or images, please contact:
Paul Eckersley, Publicity Officer, Button Books (an imprint of GMC Publications)
Tel: 044 1273 402836 Email: paul.eckersley@thegmcgroup.com

GMC Publications is distributed in North America by Publishers Group West. T: 212-614-7888; E: info@pgw.com

PRESS RELEASE
Nature Activity Book

By Alain Grée

April 2020 • RRP $12.99 • For kids aged +4
Button Books

Over 100 different nature-themed activities

This delightful nature-themed activity book will entertain children who are crazy about all things to do with the great outdoors. The pages are crammed with over 100 great activities, including dot to dot, spot the difference, coloring in, simple makes and other engaging puzzles, as well as 4 pages of stickers to be used in the book.

Fun and educational, the ***Nature Activity Book*** features beautiful, bright illustrations that will draw children in and keep them busy. All of the pages are incredibly absorbing with Alain's unmistakably rich and appealing style of illustration. And while they are enjoying the mazes, matching and counting, the games are helping them to develop a wide range of skills, including observational, conversational and motor.

About the creator:

Alain Grée is a French author and illustrator of children's books. He has had over 300 books published, which have been translated into 20 different languages. He has also worked as a children's broadcaster on French national television, produced three detective novels, ten ship navigation books and been a journalist for 20 years for *Voiles et Voiliers* (sailing ships) magazine. He is currently a graphic designer and editor for various advertising publications. Alain's main hobby is sailing. He's owned several boats since the 1970s and has crossed the Atlantic Ocean twice. He finds his sailing trips provide the perfect time out to work on new children's stories and illustrations.

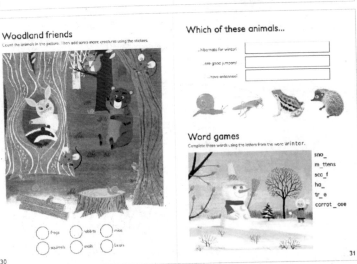

For press enquiries, review copies or images, please contact:
Paul Eckersley, Publicity Officer, Button Books (an imprint of GMC Publications)
Tel: 044 1273 402836 Email: paul.eckersley@thegmcgroup.com

GMC Publications is distributed in North America by Publishers Group West. T: 212-614-7888; E: info@pgw.com

Guess the photo

Oh dear, some of this boy's nature photographs didn't go quite as planned. Can you help him identify the animals and birds in his pictures? Write the answers in the boxes.

1.

2.

3.

4.

toucan

giraffe

lion

flamingo

Shadow fish

Match these fish to their shadows. Draw lines to connect them.

Seasonal jokes

Q: Why don't mountains get cold in winter?
A: They wear snow-caps!

Q: What do you call a dog on the beach in summer?
A: A hot dog!

Q: What goes up when the rain comes down?
A: An umbrella!

Q: What season is it when
you are on a trampoline?
A: Springtime!

Q: What falls but never gets hurt?
A: Rain!

Dragonfly maze

Help the dragonfly get through the maze to a safe pool. Avoid the frog and the toad!

Woodland walk

Can you spot five differences between these two pictures?

Springboard superstar

Who can bounce the highest off the diving board? To find out which one is the winner, do the math to find out which one has the highest score.

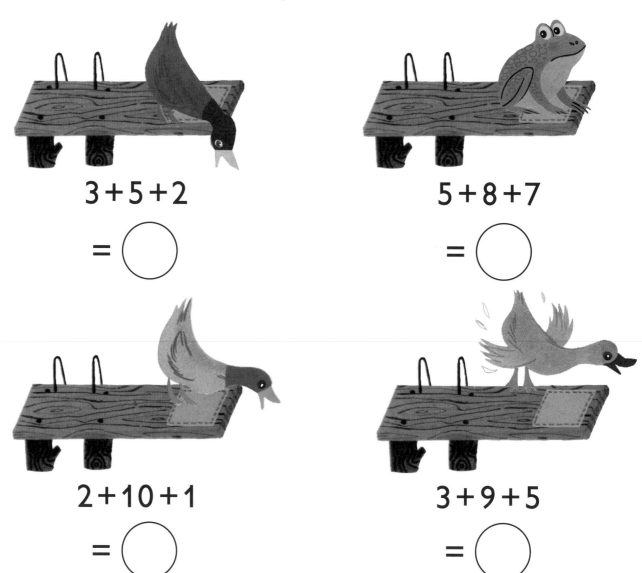

$$3 + 5 + 2$$
$$= \bigcirc$$

$$5 + 8 + 7$$
$$= \bigcirc$$

$$2 + 10 + 1$$
$$= \bigcirc$$

$$3 + 9 + 5$$
$$= \bigcirc$$

Color the shells

You can find lots of pretty seashells on the beach. Color these ones in.

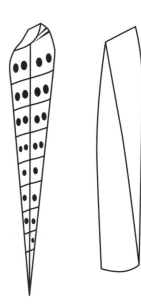

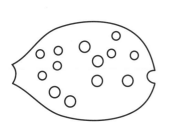

Match the feather

Which feather belongs to which bird? Match the colors and draw a line from each feather to the right bird. Which feather doesn't belong to either bird?

parrot

toucan

Odd one out

Which one of these turkeys is the odd one out?

The seasons (page 2)

spring

fall

summer

winter

Tall trees (page 5)

15 + 4 + 8 = 27 (tallest)

13 - 2 + 9 = 20

8 + 7 + 10 = 25

The caterpillar's lunch (page 4)

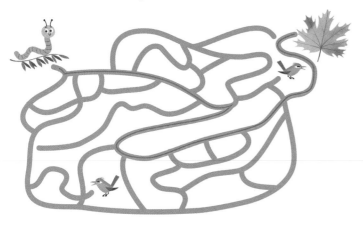

A traditional tale (page 4)

One day a beautiful but vain peacock met a sparrow on a dusty road. To show off to the sparrow, the peacock spread his lovely tail , which shone like the sun. The peacock said, "Look at me. I am dressed like a king. I am wearing all the colors of the rainbow while your feathers are as brown as dirt! What can you do?" The sparrow then spread his strong wings and flew up to the sun. "Follow me if you can," he said. But the peacock stood where he was in the dust, while the sparrow escaped into the blue sky.

The story of an apple (page 6)

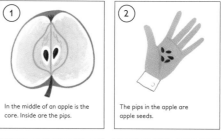

① In the middle of an apple is the core. Inside are the pips.

② The pips in the apple are apple seeds.

③ Plant an apple seed in the ground and water it.

④ The shoot grows. It forms the stem and leaves.

⑤ The plant grows into a tree.

⑥ In spring, pink and white flowers come out.

⑦ During summer, the fruits grow.

⑧ In late summer, they ripen into lovely fruit.

⑨ In fall, the apples are ready for picking.

There are 10 apples in the big basket.

Animal footprints (page 8)

The dog reaches the cozy cabin.

The rabbit reaches the woodpile.

The bird reaches the sled.

Hungry birds (page 11)

6 + 6 + 3 = 15 (ate the most)

7 + 6 - 3 = 10

10 - 2 + 6 = 14

Looking in a rock pool (page 9)

The girl might find these in a rock pool.

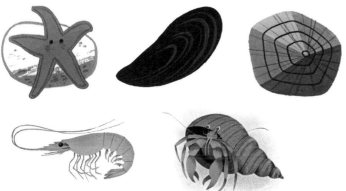

Butterfly shadows (page 12)

Nature counting (page 10)

There are 9 butterflies, 3 red butterflies,
5 yellow flowers, 3 red flowers,
2 ladybugs, and 2 bluebirds.

Matching snails (page 11)

There are 4 pairs of snails.

Springtime scene (page 13)

The weather (page 16)

sunshine

snow

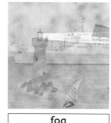
fog

rain

wind

lightning

Find the feeder (page 18)

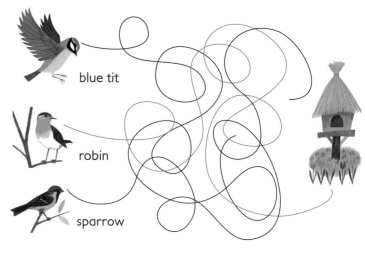

blue tit

robin

sparrow

Animal mix-up (page 18)

| pheasant | snail | frog | fox |

Sounds of nature (page 20)

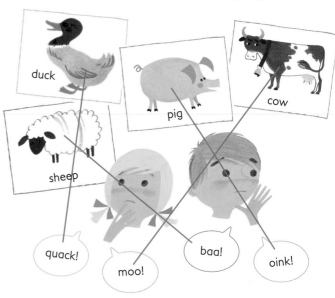

duck

pig

cow

sheep

quack!

moo!

baa!

oink!

Bird sticker fun (page 22)

Busy bees (page 24)

5 + 4 + 7 = 16 (busiest)

3 - 2 + 14 = 15

6 + 8 - 3 = 11

Garden birds (page 25)

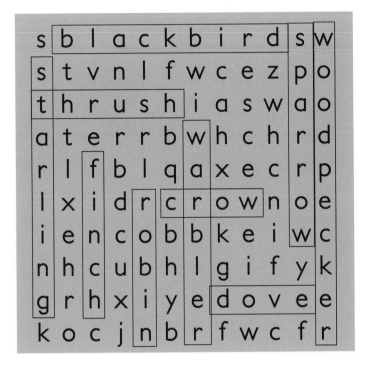

Watering the plants (page 25)

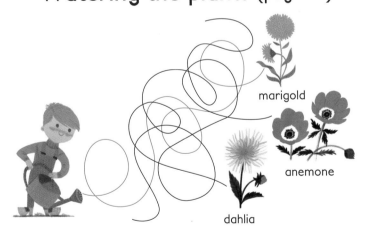

marigold

anemone

dahlia

Butterfly life cycle (page 26)

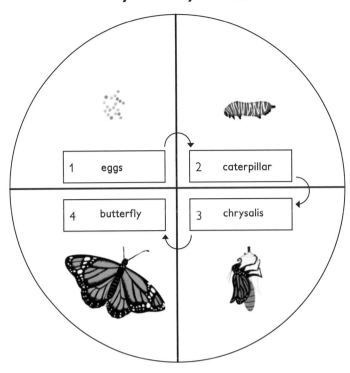

1	eggs
2	caterpillar
4	butterfly
3	chrysalis

Growing plants (page 27)

All of the following help plants grow.

Ladybug maze (page 28)

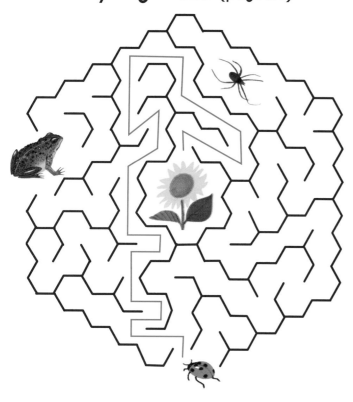

Word games (page 31)

Snow, mittens, scarf, hat, tree, carrot nose.

Crab matching (page 32)

Odd one out (page 29)

Woodland friends (page 30)

There are 3 frogs, 1 rabbit,
2 mice, 1 squirrel,
3 snails, and 1 bear.

Which of these animals...
(page 31)

...hibernate for winter?
Hedgehogs and snails

...are good jumpers?
Frogs and crickets

...have antennae?
Crickets and snails

Forest friends (page 32)

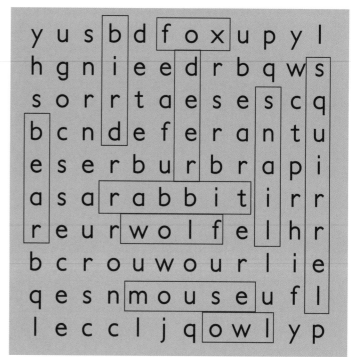

Hidden acorns (page 33)

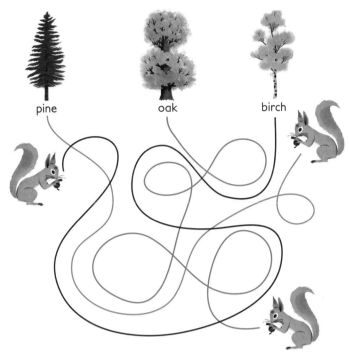

Acorns grow on oak trees.

Raking up leaves (page 34)

Where do they live? (page 35)

Wild boar, tortoises, elephants, and foxes live on the ground.

Robins, gibbons, woodpeckers, and squirrels live in trees.

Back to the hive (page 36)

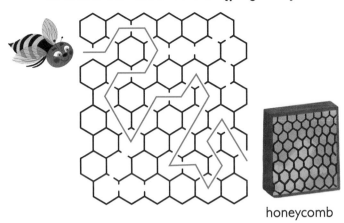

Food in nature (page 36)

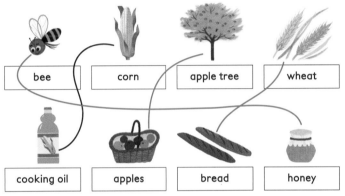

Spotting sea birds (page 37)

1. Puffin
2. Emperor penguin
3. Guillemot
4. Cormorant
5. Seagull

Summer view (page 38)

There are 27 flowers and 19 apples.

Fruit jumble (page 39)

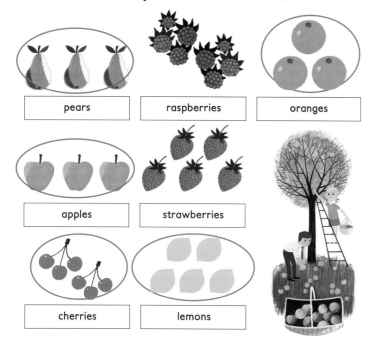

pears

raspberries

oranges

apples

strawberries

cherries

lemons

Fish and shellfish (page 40)

Sole, tuna, and cod are fish.
Shrimp, lobster, and crab are shellfish.

The old oak tree (page 41)

An old oak ⟨ tree ⟩ sat in the forest feeling very sorry for

himself. "I'm no use to anyone," he sighed. "I've got knots in my trunk,

my ⟨ branches ⟩ are all twisted and there's a pain in my fork where

the water's coming in. I'm so sad and lonely. Boo hoo!"

One dark and stormy ⟨ night ⟩, a branch blew off and left a big ⟨ hole ⟩

in the oak tree's trunk. Soon, a little ⟨ squirrel ⟩ spotted it. "Hallo, Mr. Oak! I've

been looking for somewhere to spend the ⟨ winter ⟩. That hole looks perfect for

me and my family," she said. May we stay with you?"

"Of course," said the oak tree. "It would be a pleasure." So the squirrel built her nest.

In the spring, a chirpy ⟨ robin ⟩ perched on a high branch. "Hallo, Mr. Oak!

Look at all your lovely branches! There's room for me and all my ⟨ friends ⟩

to build our nests. Please can we come and stay with you?"

"Of course," replied the old oak. Soon there were lots of ⟨ birds ⟩ in the

tree, building nests and laying their ⟨ eggs ⟩. The old oak tree was very

⟨ happy ⟩. "I guess I'm not so useless after all," he said. "And I'll never be

lonely again!"

Sink or swim? (page 43)

Penguins, goldfish, frogs, ducks, and
sea lions are good swimmers.

Fading flowers (page 44)

Lupins have the most petals.

Animal riddles (page 45)

1. Giraffe 2. Snake 3. Bee 4. Spider
5. Monkey 6. Snail

On the seashore (page 45)

Fall coloring (page 46)

There are 10 leaves on the ground.

Ocean safety (page 48)

1. b 2. a 3. b 4. b 5. a
6. b 7. a 8. b

In which season? (page 50)

...the swallow migrates

| in spring |

...we build a snowman

| in winter |

...the leaves turn brown

| in fall |

...the bear hibernates

| in winter |

...there are flowers on an apple tree

| in spring |

...the days are long and warm

| in summer |

Guess the photo (page 51)

1. Lion 2. Giraffe 3. Flamingo 4. Toucan

Shadow fish (page 52)

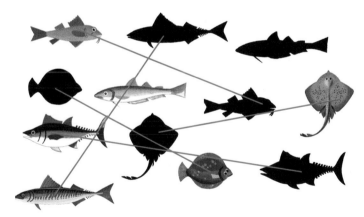

Dragonfly maze (page 53)

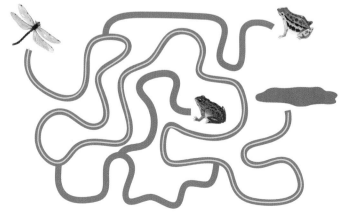

Woodland walk (page 53)

Springboard superstar (page 54)

$3 + 5 + 2 = 10$

$5 + 8 + 7 = 20$

$2 + 10 + 1 = 13$

$3 + 9 + 5 = 17$

Match the feather (page 55)

parrot

toucan

The green feather doesn't belong.

Odd one out (page 55)

First published 2020 by Button Books, an imprint of Guild of Master Craftsman Publications Ltd, Castle Place, 166 High Street, Lewes, East Sussex, BN7 1XU, UK. Text © GMC Publications Ltd, 2020. Copyright in the Work © GMC Publications Ltd, 2020. Illustrations © 2020 A.G. & RicoBel. ISBN 978 1 78708 047 8. Distributed by Publishers Group West in the United States. All rights reserved. The right of Alain Grée to be identified as the illustrator of this work has been asserted in accordance with the Copyright, Designs, and Patents Act 1988, sections 77 and 78. No part of this publication may be reproduced, stored in a retrieval system or transmitted in any form or by any means without the prior permission of the publisher and copyright owner. While every effort has been made to obtain permission from the copyright holders for all material used in this book, the publishers will be pleased to hear from anyone who has not been appropriately acknowledged and to make the correction in future reprints. The publishers and author can accept no legal responsibility for any consequences arising from the application of information, advice, or instructions given in this publication. A catalog record for this book is available from the British Library. Publisher: Jonathan Bailey. Production: Jim Bulley, Jo Pallett. Senior Project Editor: Sara Harper. Managing Art Editor: Gilda Pacitti. Designer: Ginny Zeal. Color origination by GMC Reprographics. Printed and bound in China. Warning! Choking hazard—small parts. Not suitable for children under 3 years.